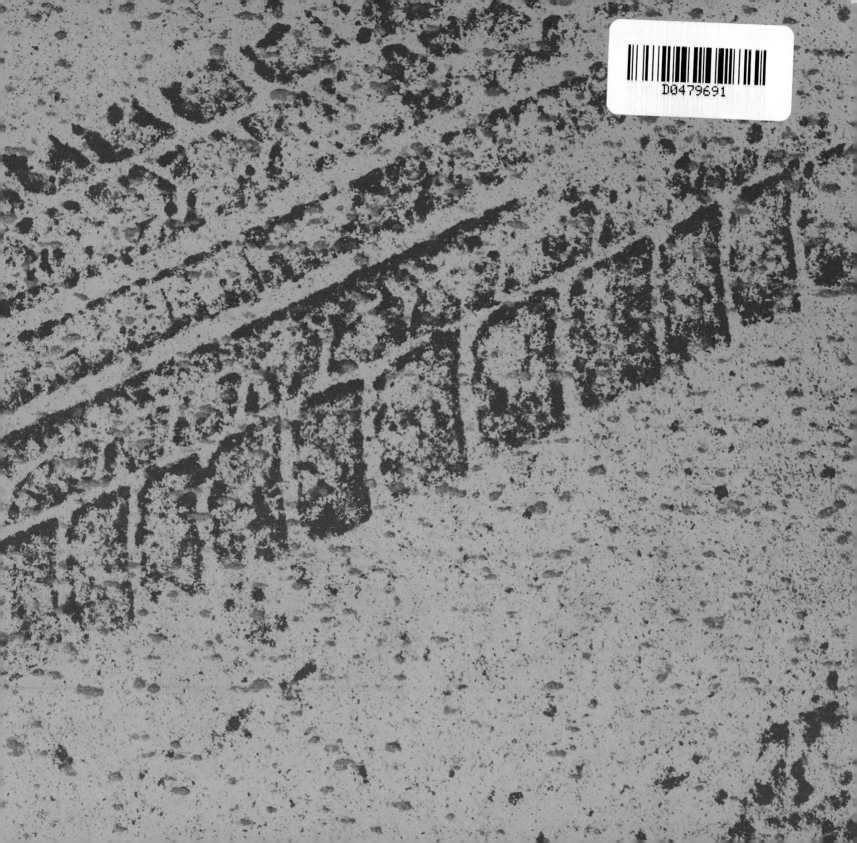

RACING DRIVER

How to drive racing cars step by step

To my godsons, Barnaby, Oscar and Ted, who might or might not be racing drivers one day.

Acknowledgments
Thanks to Annabel and Spencer for tolerating, as ever, a sometimes grumpy author.
Also to Bruce Jones, for his racing knowledge and eagle eye.

On the cover
Front: center, Laszlo Balogh/Reuters/Corbis; above left, Shutterstock.com.
Back: above left, Transtock Inc./Alamy; bottom right Elemér Sági/Dreamstime.com.

Racing Driver © 2014 Thames & Hudson Ltd, London

Created by picnic
Editorial Deborah Kespert
Design Belinda Webster

Illustrations
Damien Weighill

Text
Giles Chapman

First published in 2014 in paperback in the United States of America by
Thames & Hudson Inc., 500 Fifth Avenue, New York, New York 10110

thamesandhudsonusa.com

Library of Congress Catalog Card Number 2013950862

ISBN 978-0-500-65026-4

Printed and bound in China by Toppan Leefung

Photography
a = above; b = below; l = left; r = right; c = centre; bg = background
2–3a Shutterstock.com 2–3b Action Sports Photography/Shutterstock.com 3c
Elemér Sági/Dreamstime.com 4ar George Tiedemann/NewSport/Corbis 4bl Iryna
Rasko/Dreamstime.com 4bc Thomas Suer/DPA/Corbis 5ar Sutton Images/Corbis 4–5bg
Natursports/Dreamstime.com 6ar Philip Brown/Rex Features 6b Sutton Images/Corbis
6–7bg Kevin Fleming/Corbis 8 Thomas Suer/DPA/Corbis 9al LAT Photographic 8–9bg
Natursports/Dreamstime.com 10bl, 10br, 11al, 11ar Aston Martin 11bl Dennis Grombkowski/
Bongarts/Getty Images 11br Lars Baron/Bongarts/Getty Images 13c Sutton Images/Corbis
13bl Oliver Weiken/EPA/Corbis 12–13bg Natursports/Dreamstime.com 14cr Mercedes
Benz 14bl Phipps/Sutton Images/Corbis 15a Martin Lehmann/Dreamstime.com 15c Leo
Mason/Corbis 15br Bettmann/Corbis 14–15bg Natursports/Dreamstime.com 17 Marcelo
del Pozo/Reuters/Corbis 16–17bg Natursports/Dreamstime.com 18ar Clive Rose/JPR/Getty
Images 18bl Iryna Rasko/Dreamstime.com 19ac Sutton Images/Corbis 19cr Peter Powell/
EPA/Corbis 18–19bg Natursports/Dreamstime.com 20c George Tiedemann/NewSport/
Corbis 20br Transtock/Corbis 21bc Ron Bijlsma/Zumapress.com/Alamy Live News 20–21bg
Robert Laberge/Getty Images 22ar Action Sports Photography/Shutterstock.com 23br
Brian Czobat/Icon SMI/Corbis 22–23bg Natursports/Dreamstime.com 24cr, 24bl, 24br
George Tiedemann/NewSport/Corbis 25al George Tiedemann/GT Images/Corbis 25ac
Russell LaBounty/Icon SMI/Corbis 25ar Robert Sweeten/Corbis 25bc George Tiedemann/
NewSport/Corbis 24–25bg Action Sport Photography/Shutterstock.com 26b Thomas Suer/
DPA/Corbis 27al Ford 27ar BMW 26–27bg Natursports/Dreamstime.com 28ar Nissan 28br
Audi 29bc Peugeot 28–29bg Florian Schuh/DPA/Corbis 30cr Elemér Sági/Dreamstime.com
30bl Transtock Inc./Alamy 31al Rui Ferreira/Shutterstock.com 31ar, 31br Andres Rodriguez/
Dreamstime.com 30–31bg Patrick Poendl/Shutterstock.com 32bl Ford 32br Skoda 33al Toru
Yamanaka/AFP/Getty Images 33ar, 33bl Citroën 33br BMW 32–33bg Roberts/Shutterstock.
com 34ar Jayne Oncea/Icon SMI/Corbis 34bl Debi Pittman Wilkey/Demotix/Corbis 34br
Hideki Kimura and Kouhei Sagawa 35al Courtesy Jeff Bloch, speedcop.com/Photo by Nick
Pon 35ar Mark Phillips/Alamy 34–35bg Natursports/Dreamstime.com 36cl Maserati 36c
Phipps/Sutton Motorsport/HIP/TopFoto 36cr Sutton Images/Corbis 37al Ferrari 37ac Ahmad
Faizal Yahya/Shutterstock.com 37cr David Acosta Allely/Shutterstock.com 37bl Eagleflying/
Dreamstime.com 38cl, 38c pbpgalleries/Alamy 38cr George Tiedemann/NewSport/Corbis
39al Library of Congress, Washington, D.C. 39ar EPA b.v./Alamy 39cl Robert Laberge/Getty
Images 39c pbpgalleries/Alamy 40cl Leo Mason/Corbis 40c John Chapman 40cr V. Morfield/
Dreamstime.com 41al Michael Cole/Corbis 41ac Lor/For Picture/Corbis 41cr Peugeot 41bl
Audi 42cl, 42c ISC Archives/Getty Images 42cr Icon SMI/Corbis 43ac Ford 43ar David Allio/
Icon SMI/Corbis 43cl Lawrence Weslowski Jr/Dreamstime.com 43c Ford 44cl Science
Museum/SSPL/Getty Images 44c, 44cr, 45al Bettmann/Corbis 45ca SSC Programme Ltd.
45cr Siemens NX 45bl TopFoto 46–47bg Natursports/Dreamstime.com

RACING DRIVER

How to drive racing cars step by step

Giles Chapman

Thames & Hudson

YOUR RACING DRIVER

Would you like to be a racing driver?
Check out your training timetable here!

START IN A KART — 6

BEHIND THE WHEEL — 8

RACE TACTICS — 10

DRIVER SAFETY — 12

HISTORIC RACING — 14

FORMULA 1 RACING — 16

DRIVING AN F1 CAR — 18

RIDING THE OVAL — 20

INSIDE A STOCK CAR — 22

Do you enjoy watching fast cars speed around a track?

TIMETABLE

NASCAR RACING — 24

SUPER SEDANS — 26

INTO THE NIGHT — 28

CROSSING DESERTS — 30

RALLY EXCITEMENT — 32

CRAZY RACERS — 34

ID GUIDE — 36

DRIVING TEST — 46

INDEX — 48

Ferrari F2012

Line up on the start grid ... and you're off!

DRIVING SCHOOL

ON THE TRACK

Look out for these badges at the top of the page. They'll tell you whether you're in the classroom at driving school or practicing on the track. Just like a professional racing driver, you'll learn everything step by step.

START IN A KART

Driving a go-kart is the perfect introduction to competition racing and a huge amount of fun. Many big towns have indoor circuits in old warehouses. Why not kick-start your racing career with a thrilling karting party?

Lewis Hamilton began racing go-karts when he was eight years old. By the age of 15, he was European karting champion at the top level, with maximum points. He was spotted by the McLaren team as a future Formula 1 star.

An engine, four wheels and you!
The simplest go-karts don't have gears but practicing in a kart helps you to understand how to handle a single-seater car. You can polish your technique by placing the kart correctly on the track and choosing the best line to take a corner.

Jenson Button karting

DRIVING A GO-KART

Go-karts are designed for maximum enjoyment. They are so low to the ground that it is almost impossible to have a serious accident.

Steering column
Place your legs on either side of the steering column to drive.

Pedal controls
Press the right pedal to accelerate (go faster) and the left pedal to brake.

Wheels
The wheels are wide and small, with little tread so you can have fun twisting and turning on the track.

Engine
The single-cylinder engine is mounted behind the driver's seat and similar in power to a lawnmower.

Safety frame
Tough plastic pods at the side and front hide a steel safety frame for protection.

How to ... be a karting winner

1. Safety briefing

Pay attention to the safety briefing before the race starts. The person in charge explains the dos and don'ts, including not driving into other competitors on purpose!

2. Ready to race

Start up your engine and listen to the noise. Can you feel the tension in the air? When the track official gives the signal, stay calm and quickly stamp your foot on the accelerator.

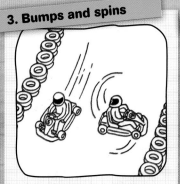

3. Bumps and spins

If you misjudge a corner, your kart might spin and you might get wedged in the side barrier. To get back in the race fast, track staff will come and help to point you forwards again.

4. You're the winner!

Concentrate hard and power towards the finish, making sure no one overtakes you at the last minute. Cross the line first and you'll receive a trophy for your efforts. Well done!

BEHIND THE WHEEL

Once you've had lots of driving practice, you're ready to try out a proper racing car. At the age of 16, you can take the wheel of a single-seater Formula 3 car like this one and train on a real race circuit.

SINGLE-SEATER

There are different kinds of single-seaters. They all have open wheels outside the bodywork and their engines are positioned in the center behind the seat so weight is distributed evenly.

1

Cockpit
This is the space where you sit to steer and control the car. It's a tight fit!

2

Roll hoop
If your car turns over the roll hoop, built into the framework, protects your head.

3

Rear spoiler
The rear spoiler is pressed down by whooshing air as you drive, increasing the car's grip on the track surface.

4

Front spoiler
The front spoiler pushes down the front of the car to give it more grip.

5

Streamlined body
The body shape makes the car aerodynamic so that it 'cheats the wind' and speeds along.

6

Mirror
Regularly check the mirror to see when a car is trying to overtake you.

FAST FACTS

☞ Car companies such as Ford and Renault run their own single-seater series. It's a brilliant way to train for Formula 1 racing.

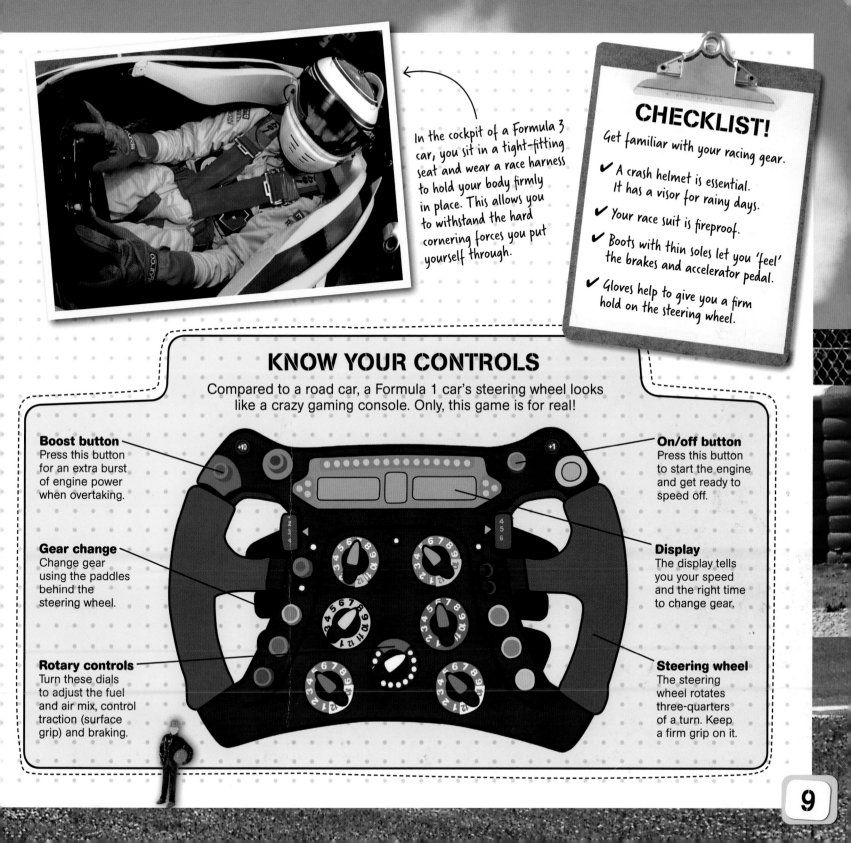

In the cockpit of a Formula 3 car, you sit in a tight-fitting seat and wear a race harness to hold your body firmly in place. This allows you to withstand the hard cornering forces you put yourself through.

CHECKLIST!

Get familiar with your racing gear.

✔ A crash helmet is essential. It has a visor for rainy days.

✔ Your race suit is fireproof.

✔ Boots with thin soles let you 'feel' the brakes and accelerator pedal.

✔ Gloves help to give you a firm hold on the steering wheel.

KNOW YOUR CONTROLS

Compared to a road car, a Formula 1 car's steering wheel looks like a crazy gaming console. Only, this game is for real!

Boost button
Press this button for an extra burst of engine power when overtaking.

Gear change
Change gear using the paddles behind the steering wheel.

Rotary controls
Turn these dials to adjust the fuel and air mix, control traction (surface grip) and braking.

On/off button
Press this button to start the engine and get ready to speed off.

Display
The display tells you your speed and the right time to change gear.

Steering wheel
The steering wheel rotates three-quarters of a turn. Keep a firm grip on it.

RACE TACTICS

Having a fast car can help you to win a motor race but brain power is just as important. You need to make full use of the track layout to keep one step ahead of your rivals and always be on the lookout for chances to overtake. Get ready to put your race tactics into action!

THE FLAG IS DOWN ...

2

MAKE A TIGHT TURN IN
By getting as close as you can to the apex, or tightest part, of the bend, you reduce the time it takes to get round the corner. At the same time, make sure you close off any gap that a driver behind you could use to jump in ahead of you.

1

GET A FLYING START
As soon as the flag drops, get your car off the starting line with plenty of acceleration. Then check you're in the right gear for the first corner. You are jostling with other cars so pay attention to how much space you have around you.

6

WIN THE RACE

You're close to the finish but don't relax and coast across the line. Concentrate hard and keep going as fast as you can. Even if no one is chasing your tail, a late challenger could roar up behind you and snatch victory. Don't let it happen!

5

ROAR DOWN THE STRAIGHT

The long straight section of the track is your best chance to show how fast your car can go. Get into top gear and press the accelerator pedal down to the floor to squeeze the maximum power from your car's engine.

DRIVER LINGO

PRACTICE LAP

This is when you try out the track before the race so you know what twists and turns to expect during the event.

3

DICE WITH OTHER CARS

Dicing is when cars fight with one another to get ahead. Quick turns of the wheel, regular checks in your mirrors and fast gear changes will help you to see off any challenges. Hand-to-eye coordination is crucial and so is lots of practice.

4

AVOID TROUBLE

At any point, a car in front of you could break down or an accident could happen. If the car ahead turns in too quickly, it could spin and you might crash into it. So always be alert for danger and be ready to take action to avoid trouble.

DRIVER SAFETY

Motor racing is exciting but it's also risky so everyone takes care to make things as safe for drivers as possible. The race track is designed to reduce the danger of an accident and your racing outfit helps to protect your body in an emergency. Let's take a closer look.

SUITED AND BOOTED

All racers must wear a helmet and an outfit of protective clothing. If your car crashes or catches fire, they could help to save you from serious injury. No one can race in a T-shirt and jeans!

Helmet
A modern helmet is light and strong. It has a hard outer shell with thick padding underneath to absorb impacts. A soft inner lining feels comfortable around your head.

Visor
The clear narrow visor, which lifts up, helps to keep your eyes focused on the track as you drive.

Radio link
A radio link built into the helmet lets the back-up team talk to you and give you updates about how the race is progressing.

Balaclava
Underneath your helmet, you wear a snug-fitting, fire-resistant balaclava. Some balaclavas cover the whole face with only eye holes for you to look through.

Race suit
Your race suit is close-fitting and all in one piece. It's made of a special material called Nomex, which helps to protect you from burns in case of a fire.

Gloves
Your gloves are also made of Nomex. They are padded but still flexible enough to let you handle the car controls easily.

Racing boots
These are made from soft leather. They have thin rubber soles so your feet won't slip off the pedals when you're driving under pressure.

Race track safety

Metal barriers lined with tires hug the edges of the circuit. When a driver crashes into them, they absorb the car's energy and stop it from leaving the track. This helps to keep the crowd safe.

MARSHAL
A person standing around the circuit who watches the race and reports on anything that might turn into a risk for a driver.

This graveled section of the track edge is called the run-off area. It is often found at tight corners. A driver in trouble can steer into the gravel, which helps the car to stop.

Here's a dangerous situation – a car has just caught fire after being refuelled. Luckily the pit crew are trained to deal with emergencies like this. There are also fire engines on standby during every race.

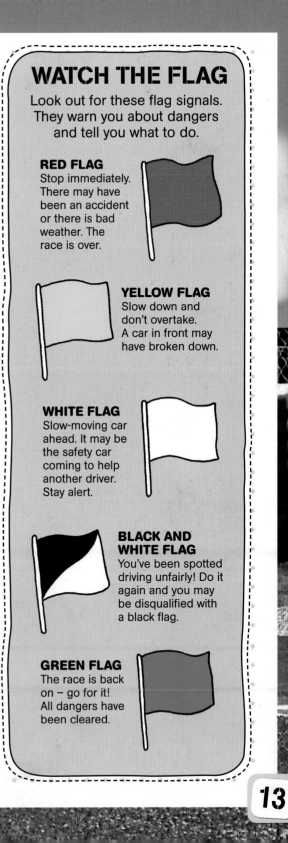

WATCH THE FLAG

Look out for these flag signals. They warn you about dangers and tell you what to do.

RED FLAG
Stop immediately. There may have been an accident or there is bad weather. The race is over.

YELLOW FLAG
Slow down and don't overtake. A car in front may have broken down.

WHITE FLAG
Slow-moving car ahead. It may be the safety car coming to help another driver. Stay alert.

BLACK AND WHITE FLAG
You've been spotted driving unfairly! Do it again and you may be disqualified with a black flag.

GREEN FLAG
The race is back on – go for it! All dangers have been cleared.

HISTORIC RACING

Would you like to own an old racing car and take part in a historic racing competition? Even though old racers don't go as fast as modern ones, you still need expert driving skills. That's because they are tricky to control and there are no electronic gadgets on the dashboard to help you out.

⭐ MERCEDES-BENZ

During the late 1930s, the Mercedes-Benz W125 car ruled European Grand Prix racing. In 1937, W125 drivers took the top four places of the European Championship. Today, only five of these cars remain. They are extremely valuable.

Mercedes-Benz W125

rear aerofoil

Ferrari 312 F1

⭐ FERRARI

How about taking this fabulous Formula 1 Ferrari, driven by Jacky Ickx in 1968, out on the track? It has a 3-liter V12 engine and can reach speeds of up to 193 miles per hour. It was the first F1 Ferrari to have a rear aerofoil, helping to keep the car firmly gripped to the ground.

Did you know?

The most expensive car on the planet is a 1954 Mercedes-Benz W196. It was once raced by the Argentinian driver Juan Manuel Fangio. It costs about $33 million to buy.

8

⭐ ALFA ROMEO

In the late 1960s, this Alfa Romeo with its lightweight body shell was successful in touring-car racing worldwide. You can race it today against other similar cars such as Minis and BMWs. It drives like a normal road car but responds to your actions more quickly.

112

☞ In the Mille Miglia race, you can drive your old car on Italian roads, just like racing drivers did in the 1950s.

☞ Join the Vintage Sports Car Club of America and you can take part in historic races all over the country.

☞ Even though you're racing old cars, you still need to wear the latest protective gear to stay safe on the track.

Shelby/
AC Cobra

⭐ COBRA

The AC Cobra is a classic sports car. It has a body designed in the UK and contains a powerful American Ford V8 engine. You'll find it fiercely fast to drive but once you get used to its power, you'll love it!

4

This 'Competition For Horseless Carriages' was the first ever 'race' for cars. It took place in 1894 in France between Paris and Rouen. The winner was Albert Lamâitre. He took 6 hours and 48 minutes to drive the 79 mile course at an average speed of 12 miles per hour.

FORMULA 1 RACING

Formula 1 (also known as F1) racing is popular in Europe and countries such as Japan and Australia. To be a winner, you must have skill and dedication as well as a super-fast, reliable racing car. You also need support from a back-up team, which can include up to 700 people!

A huge event
F1 teams travel over 90,000 miles every year to attend races. They use trucks and aircraft to carry drivers and cars. When the teams arrive, they book out hundreds of hotel rooms.

IN THE PITS
During a race, a driver makes regular pit stops for wheel changes as their tires wear out. The pits are next to the race track alongside a garage workshop. A highly experienced team, called the pit crew, are on standby for you all the time, ready to fix any problems.

How to … make a pit stop

1. Get the alert

When you hear on the radio to make a pit stop, slow down and pull off the track. Press the pit lane speed-limiter button to make the car travel at the right speed, then stop by your garage.

2. Keep it running

You'll see a person holding a sign while the pit crew work on your car. Keep one foot on the brake pedal and the gears in neutral. At the same time, rev the engine a little so it doesn't stall.

3. Go, go, go …

As soon as the pit crew finish their work, press the accelerator pedal and zoom away. Turn off the pit lane speed limiter as you cross the exit line and get straight back on the track!

Wheel-on crew
The 'wheel-on' crew put on a new wheel and tighten the nuts to secure it.

Power tools
These pipes deliver compressed air to the wheel guns that are needed to undo the wheel nuts.

Lollipop baton
A lollipop-shaped sign with instructions reminds you what to do while you wait.

Wheel-off crew
A wheel change takes 3.5 seconds. The 'wheel-off' crew undo the nuts that hold the wheel in place and take off the wheel.

DRIVER LINGO

LOLLIPOP MAN
This is the name for the man who holds the big instruction sign. His first job is to tell you exactly where to stop.

Sit tight
Your job is to stay calm and keep the engine running. A team member will wipe your visor so you can see clearly.

Arm signal
When the job is finished, a team member signals with his arms. This tells the lollipop man to wave you back onto the track.

DRIVING AN F1 CAR

So you've finished your practice laps and competed for your position on the start grid. Are you ready for the race of your life? You'll be driving at speeds touching 180 miles per hour for up to two hours. Stay focused!

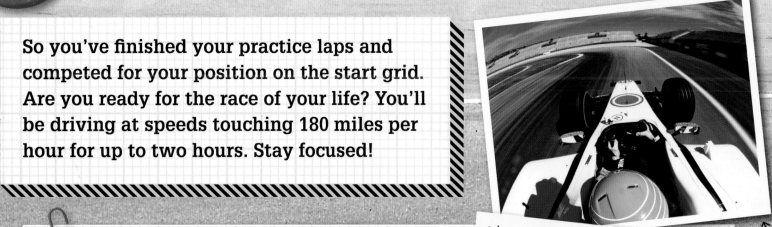

AROUND THE CIRCUIT

A race circuit is a one-way, never-ending route so there's no need for a road map. It's full of twists and turns to keep you on your toes. This is a race circuit shown from above.

When you approach a tight corner, begin your 'turn in' — that's the point when you steer your car into the curve. Drivers use their judgment to pick the right moment to turn in. Don't be scared. All it takes is practice.

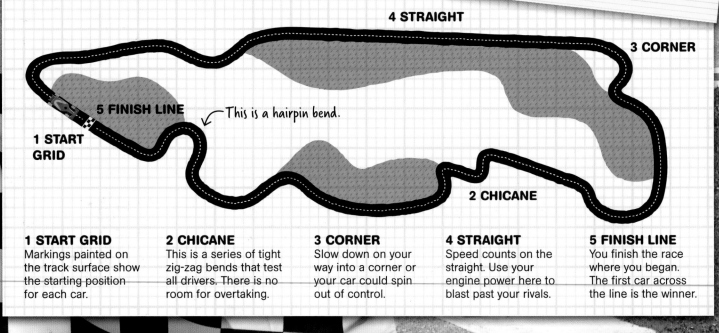

This is a hairpin bend.

4 STRAIGHT

3 CORNER

5 FINISH LINE

1 START GRID

2 CHICANE

1 START GRID
Markings painted on the track surface show the starting position for each car.

2 CHICANE
This is a series of tight zig-zag bends that test all drivers. There is no room for overtaking.

3 CORNER
Slow down on your way into a corner or your car could spin out of control.

4 STRAIGHT
Speed counts on the straight. Use your engine power here to blast past your rivals.

5 FINISH LINE
You finish the race where you began. The first car across the line is the winner.

Ferrari F2012

The race goes ahead even if it is raining. Your challenge is to keep the car rolling on the wet slippery track while driving through the spray thrown up by other cars.

Formula 1 teams bring along different kinds of tires, including wet weather ones, so you have tires that suit every type of track condition. They are warmed up before the race to make them soft and sticky for extra grip.

How to ... overtake on a corner

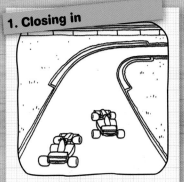

1. Closing in

The driver in front is trying to hold you off as he approaches the corner. He moves out of line! As you start closing in, look for your chance to steer into any gap he leaves.

2. Braking point

You're driving at high speed. Pick your moment to press the brakes, leaving it as late as you can. Draw level with the other car so the driver has no chance to cut across your path.

3. Power out

The moment you have the chance to power ahead, take it. You must be quick because even a slower car can pull ahead again if you're on the outside of a corner.

FAST FACTS

☞ Formula 1 drivers race over a yearly season, scoring 25 points for each win. Only the top ten finishers in a race score points. If you come tenth, you score one point.

☞ As well as fellow racing drivers, a Formula 1 team includes mechanics, engineers, designers and even a team chef!

RIDING THE OVAL

IndyCar racing is the US rival to Formula 1 racing but it's a different driving experience. The cars are heavier and they slide more easily. The races are also longer. If you're good at concentrating for long periods and extremely fit, then you could lead the pack!

2011 Dallara Honda

DRIVER LINGO

INDY 500
This is short for Indianapolis 500, a famous 500-mile IndyCar race that happens once a year in Indiana, USA.

Danica Patrick is the only woman to have won an IndyCar series race. In 2009, in the Indy 500, she finished third — the highest placing for a woman ever. Her dad drives her motorhome to competitions and her mom runs her office.

Take it to the limit
An Indy car has open wheels with a huge turbocharged engine. It reaches a high speed so you'll take a corner at 150 miles per hour. Get ready to feel the force!

INDYCAR RACING TRACKS

IndyCar races take place on different types of track. About half of the circuits are oval in shape. Almost all of the venues are in North America.

Texas Motor Speedway, Texas

Sonoma Raceway, California

St Petersburg Circuit, Florida

OVAL CIRCUIT

On an oval track, you can make only left-hand turns. The shape is perfect for the crowd because it can see all the action down the straight and at the corners at once. The Texas Motor Speedway is 1.5 miles long.

RACE CIRCUIT

It's a real challenge driving on a specially built race circuit. There are lots of twists and turns in both directions to steer round as well as long straights to roar down. These tracks are sometimes called 'road courses'.

STREET CIRCUIT

Imagine racing through city streets, whizzing past shops and offices. Sometimes, IndyCar races are held on normal roads that have been closed off to traffic. The crowd goes wild and the atmosphere is electric. This Florida street circuit stretches for 1.8 miles.

Watch out for the safety car. When there is a crash or breakdown, a safety car comes out onto the track and carefully leads the other cars round the circuit. If you see the safety car during a race, make sure you slow down immediately.

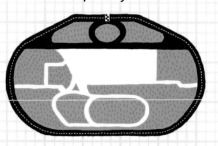

FAST FACTS

☞ When racing on a superspeedway, change your steel brakes to carbon-fiber ones to give you extra stopping power.

☞ IndyCar races have a rolling start. Drivers follow the safety car slowly until it pulls off the track to let the racing begin properly.

INSIDE A STOCK CAR

Stock car racing, known as NASCAR in the USA, is a sport for the bravest drivers. Shoving other cars out of the way as you power through the pack is an important skill. The car you drive is extremely tough and built to put up with all the bashes and bumps.

WHAT IS A STOCK CAR?

'Stock' is another word for 'standard' or 'production'. In NASCAR races, stock cars share the same overall shape as standard production cars you see on the road, but inside they're highly specialized speed machines in three sections: chassis, frame and body.

There's just one seat inside the car for the driver. The noise during a race would be deafening without a helmet on!

CHASSIS

The chassis is the base frame of a car. It carries the engine and the transmission, which is the mechanism that turns the wheels. The big V8 engine in a stock car is basic but powerful, and the car has a four-speed manual gearbox. A steel 'firewall' separates you from the engine and the fuel tank for extra safety.

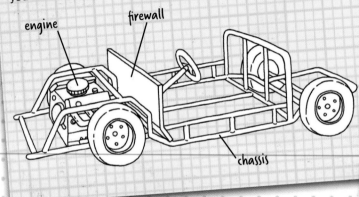

engine   firewall

chassis

SAFETY FRAME

The super-strong safety frame slots onto the chassis. The central section is a tough tubular steel cage designed to protect you in an accident. Your car's body fits over the safety frame. The doors don't open but there is an escape hatch in the roof to climb out of in an emergency. The headlights on your car are fake too!

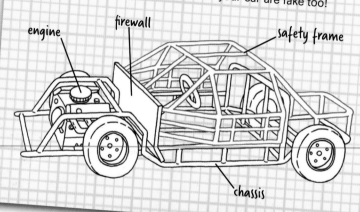

engine   firewall   safety frame

chassis

NASCAR DIARY

NASCAR events take place over a whole weekend with hundreds of thousands of fans watching. This is a typical race day.

Saturday 10 AM

PRACTICE LAP:
52 SECONDS

Qualifying

After practicing hard on Friday, you qualify for your starting position on the track Saturday morning with timed laps. Get a fast time and you'll be near the front. Fingers crossed that it doesn't rain, because you can't race in wet weather.

Saturday 12 PM

They're off!

Forty-five minutes before the race begins you meet the crowd. Then you head to the start grid. The grand marshal shouts 'drivers, start your engines'. Run your engine for three minutes, make three laps around the track to build pace, then go!

Saturday 5 PM

Meet the press

When the race is over and you've won, celebrate with burnouts – that's spinning your wheels while the car is still to create lots of smoke. Afterwards it's time for TV interviews to let everyone at home know the secrets of your winning technique!

There's a real party atmosphere at NASCAR races espcecially when the winner is announced. Here Matt Kenseth and the Joe Gibbs Racing Team celebrate their Sprint Cup race victory at the Las Vegas Motor Speedway, Nevada.

SILLY SEASON

This is the time of year when teams change drivers and crew to improve performance. It gets the fans talking!

DRIVER LINGO

NASCAR RACING

NASCAR is one of the most popular sports in the USA. You race around an oval circuit at about 180 miles per hour, just inches apart from the other cars. It's a real test of survival and nerves. Even while your rivals are bumping into you, try to keep cool.

Dale Earnhardt was probably the greatest ever NASCAR driver, winning 76 races in his 26-year career. Stock car racing is dangerous and Dale died in a race crash in 2001 but his son Dale Earnhardt, Jr. continues to race today.

It's all action!
NASCAR events are usually held inside stadiums in front of up to 250,000 people. The atmosphere is electrifying. Show daring in your driving style and you'll get huge cheers from the crowds.

Dodge Charger

DRIVER LINGO

DAYTONA 500
This is a world-famous NASCAR race held once a year at the Daytona International Speedway in Florida.

RACE TACTICS

The action is fast and furious. Follow these tactics to cross the finish line first.

GET A FAST START
Stock cars are quite evenly matched on engine power, so you need quick reactions to make a rapid start from the top of the banked, or sloped, edge of the circuit and move up the field. There's no time to hang around.

AVOID A PILE-UP
Accidents happen all the time. Avoiding one isn't easy because impatient drivers nudge you out of the way, sending your car up the banking. The trick is to make sure you nudge the car in front before the one behind nudges you.

BUMP YOUR RIVALS
The technique in this photo is called bump-drafting. Tuck your car behind the one in front and use the slipstream to give you extra speed. Then give the car in front a gentle shove out of the way so you can fill the space. Hold your nerve!

FAST FACTS

☞ NASCAR stands for the National Association for Stock Car Auto Racing. The first race was in 1948 with only American-made cars.

☞ Officials wave flags to give out messages. A white flag means one lap to go. A black flag gives you a penalty.

☞ One car can wear out as many as 36 tires in a single race. For long races, the tires have an extra lining for safety.

Chevrolet Monte Carlo

SUPER SEDANS

In 2005, the modern World Touring Car Championship (WTCC) was created. It gave different types of drivers the chance to get on a track and race road cars, such as sedans and hatchbacks, similar to the ones your family might own.

Road cars become racers

In touring car racing, you drive a normal road car that has been modified inside. To win, you need to be good at handling tight corners and able to keep calm under pressure as your rivals will be hot on your tail!

CHECKLIST!

Touring cars are exciting to race for lots of reasons.

✔ They are easy to learn to drive — you operate them like road cars.

✔ They challenge your handling skills as you twist, turn and brake.

✔ They improve your reactions.

✔ They provide fun for the crowd!

Some countries have their own touring car championships. This one is taking place in Germany. The cars on the track include Audis, BMWs and Mercedes-Benz. These German-built cars are far more powerful than the cars used in the World Touring Car Championship races.

CHOOSE YOUR CAR

To keep the racing varied, you can choose the car you want to drive. All have four doors, powerful engines, six-speed gearboxes and can reach speeds of up to 150 miles per hour.

Ford Focus

⭐ REAR-WHEEL DRIVE

The engine in this BMW 320i sends its power to the two back wheels. If you take a corner too quickly and start losing grip on the track, you're oversteering. Don't turn the steering wheel quite so hard.

BMW 320i

⭐ FRONT-WHEEL DRIVE

The engine in this Ford Focus sends its power to the two front wheels. If you take a corner too quickly and start to lose control, you're understeering. Turn the steering wheel harder.

TOURING CAR RACER COCKPIT

The cockpit of a touring car racer is based on the inside of a road car with a few important differences. This picture shows you a racer cockpit from the side.

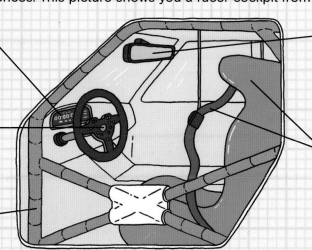

An electronic display shows you exactly how the car is performing and includes a lap timer.

Controls for windshield wipers and lights are on your steering wheel instead of the dashboard.

Roll bars help to protect you if you crash.

An extra-wide rear-view mirror allows you to check on the action behind.

Your seat has a wide head restraint and harness for extra safety.

Test yourself!

Q: What equipment will you be glad to have in your racer if you have an accident?

A: The roll bars. They will stop the car's bodywork from pressing down on you if the car rolls over.

INTO THE NIGHT

In endurance racing, the challenge is to drive the longest distance you can in a set amount of time. The most famous endurance race is the Le Mans 24 Hours which takes place once a year in France. You're on the road day and night. Have you got what it takes?

This is Gunnar Jeannette, an American driver born in 1982. At the age of 18, he became the youngest person ever to finish the Le Mans 24 Hours race. Away from the track, Gunnar has made over 1,000 skydives!

Take turns

Part of the race is on a motor racing circuit and the rest on country roads closed to traffic. It's impossible to drive the whole distance on your own, so each team has several drivers who race the same car in 'shifts'. When it's your turn, jump in as quickly as you can and drive hard and fast!

Audi R15

How to ... win the Le Mans 24 Hours

1. Rolling start

3 PM

In the afternoon, get ready for a rolling start. The winner, 24 hours later, will be the car that has covered the most laps. The noise from the engines is deafening as the pack roars off.

2. Pit stop

2 AM

When you need more fuel, pull into the pits. Stop here for repairs too but not at the same time. Tell the crew how your car is performing so the team can keep it in tip-top condition.

3. Change driver

8 AM

You also change drivers in the pits. Get out of the car quickly. When you're not behind the wheel, make sure that you eat, rest and relax so that you feel refreshed for the next shift.

4. Race over

3 PM

The next day, on the final lap, race towards the finish line to victory. The race marshals will wave flags to congratulate you and the crowd will cheer wildly. You've beaten everyone!

Peugeot 908

FAST FACTS

☞ No one is allowed to drive for longer than four hours at a time. Your team manager will plan who is behind the wheel next.

☞ There are at least three drivers in each team. Each one is extremely fit, has high-speed driving skills and lots of stamina.

CROSSING DESERTS

When you race off-road, it's a battle against the clock and the landscape. This is your chance to take part in the Dakar Rally – an adventure through desert sands across different countries. There are categories for cars, trucks and even motorbikes. Which of these vehicles will you choose?

⭐ OFF-ROAD RACER

This Mitsubishi racer won the Dakar Rally from Europe to Africa seven times in a row. It's four-wheel drive and has a tough engine with lots of pulling power. Long-travel suspension cushions the car as it flies off sand dunes.

Mitsubishi Pajero Montero

Baja 1000 dune buggy

⭐ DUNE BUGGY

A dune buggy is designed to get you through sand. It has big, powered back wheels and tires for grip, and un-powered front ones for bouncing over obstacles. It also has a strong cage to protect you and a powerful engine to push you forwards.

DRIVER LINGO

RALLY RAID

This is the name given to off-road racing often across different countries. A rally raid can take up to 15 days.

Your race could be over if you get stuck in the sand. Make small steering movements to left and right. Accelerate gently backwards and forwards. The tires should 'bite' and then you can climb out of the sand.

Hummer H3 prototype

Kamaz 4 x 4 truck

⭐ SPECIAL BUILD RACER

Would you like to build your own special car? This one began life as a Hummer H3 road car. It was given lightweight bodywork, massive tires and changed from four-wheel to two-wheel drive to make it easier to handle in deep sand and on stones.

CHECKLIST!

It's going to be a long, hot trip. Here's what you need to take.

✔ A co-driver to read maps and check the compass for directions.

✔ Water to drink and for the engine.

✔ Spare wheels and tires.

✔ A satellite phone to call for back-up in an emergency.

⭐ RACING TRUCK

The sheer size, weight and power of this Russian four-wheel drive truck makes it almost unstoppable. But you've got to have the right skills to handle it and know exactly when to brake. Practice driving a military tank first!

RALLY EXCITEMENT

When you take part in a rally, you drive across incredible landscapes on different types of terrain, such as gravel, mud, snow and ice. The World Rally Championship includes over a dozen rallies held throughout the year. Are you skilled enough to win one?

CHECKLIST!

Before the rally, check out the route with your co-driver.

✔ Drive along at a slow speed.

✔ Decide how to tackle tricky corners.

✔ Work out your top speeds between obstacles.

✔ Note the types of terrain and how best to deal with them.

TAKE IT TO THE EXTREME ...

1

SPLASH THROUGH A RIVER
You're likely to cross a river or a shallow lake, so make sure you know how your car will react. Pick your route carefully, trying not to lose speed. Concentrate hard and switch on your windshield wipers.

2

SIDEWAYS IN THE SNOW
In snow and ice, a four-wheel drive car has an advantage over a two-wheel drive car. In a two-wheel drive car your wheels might slide. Turn the steering wheel carefully to avoid spinning or swerving off the track.

6

THE CROWD GOES WILD!
The crowd will love to see your rally driving skills in action. They gather at the finish line and also at spots where they're likely to see your car acrobatics at their finest.

DRIVER LINGO

SPECIAL STAGE
A challenging timed section of a rally on a road closed to the public, for example a mountain pass or rough forest trail.

5

KICK UP A CLOUD OF DUST
In a hot dry country, your wheels throw up huge clouds of dust. Luckily though, you won't have to drive through dust clouds made by rivals because you tackle each stage of a rally one car at a time, racing against the clock.

4

JUMP AND BOUNCE
There are no prizes for being too cautious. Drive fast and enjoy leaping off the ground and crashing back down again when you hit the brow of a hill. The car can take it – it's built to withstand a battering.

3

FLY OVER MUD
Muddy ground with bumps and dips really take it out of your car and can be tricky to handle. Expert drivers use their bottoms as a sensor to know where to point the car next – they 'feel' the mix of hard and soft ground through the seat! Why not give it a go?

CRAZY RACERS

So you've learned how to drive well-known types of racing cars but what if you want to go wild and enjoy a totally different kind of driving experience? Here are a few crazy vehicles you can try out. Which is your favorite?

Dodge funny car

Swamp buggy

⭐ FUNNY CAR
This type of car is used for drag racing, which is a popular sport in the USA. You race at high speed against a rival over a short distance. When you cross the finish line, set off the parachute to slow down.

solar panel

Tokai solar car

⭐ SWAMP BUGGY
A swamp buggy is an amphibious car, which means it can travel through water as well as on land. It has a powerful engine and special wheels to race through murky bogs filled with slimy plants, twigs and logs.

⭐ SOLAR CAR
Every year in Australia, a long-distance road race called the World Solar Challenge takes place. Your fuel is sunshine! Solar panels convert the sunshine to electricity that powers your car.

Two old bangers

⭐ DEMOLITION DERBY

You can enjoy big thrills entering old cars into demolition derbies. Just remove all the windows and add a safety cage. Then barge around, bashing rivals out of the way until your car gets wrecked and you can't carry on. Great fun!

SPEEDYCOP.COM

'LeMons' budget racer

⭐ UPSIDE-DOWN CAR

This car has been built to look like you're driving it upside down! It's taking part in the US 'LeMons' race, where every car entered must cost under $500 to buy. A 'lemon' is slang for a useless car.

How to ... ride a Segway

1. What is a Segway?

A Segway is a two-wheeled vehicle for one person powered by electricity. You ride it standing up like a scooter. To move forwards, lean your body forwards. Push the handlebars to turn left or right.

2. Get started

Riding a Segway is easy once you know how. An instructor teaches you to use your own sense of balance to tell the Segway which way to go. You must wear knee and elbow pads and a helmet for protection.

3. Go for a ride

Then you'll head off on a forest trail or off-road track. Don't try to overtake – the roads aren't wide enough. Instead, enjoy a follow-my-leader adventure. Riding a Segway is a great chance to practice your steering technique.

FORMULA 1 CARS

Formula 1 racing started in 1950 and is the world's leading type of motor sport. Up to 500 million people watch it on TV every year. The pressure on teams and drivers to win is huge.

MASERATI 250F

Country: Italy
Years: 1954 to 1960
Engine size: 2490 cc*
Top speed: about 180 miles per hour
Races won: 8
Famous driver: Juan Manuel Fangio

⭐ Early Formula 1 cars had their engines ahead of the driver. Maserati battled with Ferrari, Mercedes-Benz, Talbot and Vanwall cars, among others, to rule the sport.

LOTUS 25

Country: UK
Years: 1962 to 1967
Engine size: 1498 cc
Top speed: about 140 miles per hour
Races won: 14
Famous driver: Jim Clark

⭐ In 1963, Scottish driver Jim Clark became World Champion in this Lotus. The car was nicknamed 'The Bathtub' because of its laid-back driving position.

MCLAREN MP4/1

Country: UK
Years: 1981 to 1983
Engine size: 2993 cc
Top speed: about 200 miles per hour
Races won: 6
Famous driver: John Watson

⭐ This car increased driver safety because its body was made from a strong carbon-fibre material. All today's Formula 1 cars are inspired by it.

* CC stands for cubic centimeters, a measurement that tells you the size of the engine. Lots of 'cc' means you have a big, powerful motor.

FERRARI F2004

MOST WINS

Country: Italy
Years: 2004 to 2005
Engine size: 2997 cc
Top speed: 217 miles per hour
Races won: 15
Famous driver: Michael Schumacher

⭐ Ferrari's F2004 is thought to be the fastest F1 car of all time. It started 12 times in pole position (first on the start grid) and still holds many lap records today.

BRAWN BGP 001

Country: UK
Years: 2009
Engine size: 2400 cc
Top speed: over 200 miles per hour
Races won: 8
Famous driver: Jenson Button

⭐ The Brawn BGP 001 ruled the 2009 season after its drivers finished both first and second in their first ever race. The car made Jenson Button World Champion.

DID YOU KNOW?
Formula 1 teams battle each other to win the World Constructors' Championship. This is awarded to the team whose drivers score the most points throughout the season.

RED BULL RB8

Country: UK
Years: 2012
Engine size: 2400 cc
Top speed: over 200 miles per hour
Races won: 7
Famous driver: Sebastian Vettel

⭐ In 2013, Red Bull won its fourth Formula 1 Constructors' Championship. In that same year, Sebastian Vettel won the drivers' title – his fourth in a row!

Michael Schumacher is the most successful Formula 1 driver ever. He won 91 F1 races and became World Champion seven times between 1991 and his retirement in 2012. Everyone admired his dedication, hard work and top-class driving skills.

INDY CARS

Indy car racing is North America's top-level race series for single-seater, open-wheel cars. It's been around since 1904. The Indy cars of today look quite similar to Formula 1 cars.

MILLER 122

Country: USA
Years: 1923 to 1929
Engine size: 1980 cc
Top speed: about 141 miles per hour
INDY 500 wins: 6
Famous driver: Tommy Milton

⭐ This was one of the first purpose-built racing cars. It was a tight fit for the driver – the cockpit was just 18 inches wide. Miller engines powered 12 Indy 500-winning cars.

KURTIS-KRAFT OFFENHAUSER

MOST POWERFUL

Country: USA
Years: 1948 to 1961
Engine size: 4179 cc
Top speed: over 143 miles per hour
INDY 500 wins: 6
Famous driver: Bill Vukovich

⭐ Between 1950 and 1955, a Kurtis-Kraft racing car with an Offenhauser engine won the Indy 500 six times. The engine was set to one side for taking corners.

PENSKE CHEVROLET PC18

Country: UK
Years: 1989
Engine size: 3430 cc
Top speed: over 211 miles per hour
INDY 500 wins: 1
Famous driver: Emerson Fittipaldi

⭐ A Penske Chevrolet won the Indy 500 two years in a row – in 1988 with the PC17 and in 1989 with the PC18. Penske cars have competed in Indy racing since 1978.

In 1911, Ray Harroun won the first Indy 500 race in a Marmon Wasp. The car averaged 76 miles per hour and saw off competition from 39 other racers. It was fitted with the first ever rear-view mirror to help keep rivals at bay!

DALLARA HONDA DW12

Country: Italy
Years: 2012
Engine size: 2200 cc
Top speed: about 230 miles per hour
INDY 500 wins: 1
Famous driver: Dario Franchitti

⭐ This car was the first new Indy car design since 2003. Its driver Dario Franchitti won the 2012 Indy 500 after the car in the lead changed 34 times!

DALLARA OLDSMOBILE

Country: USA, Italy
Years: 2001
Engine size: 4000 cc
Top speed: over 224 miles per hour
INDY 500 wins: 4
Famous driver: Hélio Castroneves

⭐ The engine for this car came from the USA but the chassis was made in Italy. Dallara has been the leading supplier of Indy cars since 1988.

PANOZ G-FORCE TOYOTA

Country: USA, UK, Japan
Years: 2002 to 2006
Engine size: 3500 cc
Top speed: 230 miles per hour
INDY 500 wins: 1
Famous driver: Gil De Ferran

⭐ In 2003, there was victory for this car at the Indy 500 on its first ever race. Brazilian driver Gil De Ferran averaged 224 miles per hour to hold off his rivals.

DID YOU KNOW?
In 1952, Troy Ruttman became the youngest ever Indy 500 winner, aged just 22. It was the only time he stood on the podium to take the trophy.

SPORTS RACERS

A sports racer is a two-seater sports car usually with its wheels covered by the bodywork. Races can last for a whole day, so two people share the driving to get round the circuit safely.

BENTLEY SPEED SIX

Country: UK
Years: 1929 to 1930
Engine size: 6597 cc
Top speed: 125 miles per hour
Number made: 182
Famous driver: Henry 'Tim' Birkin

⭐ In 1930, the boss of Bentley Motors raced a Bentley Speed Six from France to England against a train for a bet. He won but was fined for racing on French roads!

PORSCHE 962

Country: Germany
Years: 1985 to 1989
Engine size: 2994 cc
Top speed: 211 miles per hour
Number made: 150
Famous driver: Derek Bell

⭐ Together with the Porsche 956, the 962 won 232 races in 12 years, including seven Le Mans 24 Hours race victories. It starts with a key just like a road car.

FORD GT40

Country: UK
Years: 1964 to 1969
Engine size: up to 6997 cc
Top speed: 186 miles per hour
Number made: 107
Famous driver: Jacky Ickx

⭐ The GT40 got its name because it was designed for Gran Turismo racing and was only 40 inches high. It is one of the world's lowest-to-the-ground cars.

JAGUAR D-TYPE

Country: UK
Years: 1954 to 1957
Engine size: 3442 cc
Top speed: 180 miles per hour
Number made: 71
Famous driver: Ron Flockhart

⭐ In the 1950s, a Jaguar D-type won the Le Mans 24 Hours race three times. The car was fast and had a fin behind the driver to make it stable at high speed.

AUDI R10 TDI

Country: Germany
Years: 2006 to 2008
Engine size: 5500 cc
Top speed: 204 miles per hour
Number made: about 12
Famous driver: Frank Biela

⭐ This wide flat car became a legend when it won the first ever race it was entered into. It has a diesel engine and metal rollover hoops to protect the driver.

PEUGEOT 908 HDi FAP

FASTEST

Country: France
Years: 2007 to 2010
Engine size: 5486 cc
Top speed: 212 miles per hour
Number made: about 12
Famous driver: Marc Gené

⭐ In 2009, this diesel-powered car won the Le Mans 24 Hours race with a team of three drivers. When the car crossed the finish line, the crowd went wild.

Danish Tom Kristensen is one of the greatest sports car racing drivers of all time. He's won the Le Mans 24 Hours race nine times — seven times driving Audis, once driving a Bentley and once driving a Porsche.

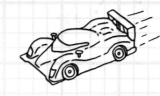

NASCAR POWER

In the early days, people raced in NASCAR events using ordinary cars like those on American roads. Today, the cars are specialized machines that can travel at over 180 miles per hour.

HUDSON HORNET

Country: USA
Year introduced: 1951
Vehicle type: stock car
Engine size: 5047 cc
Top speed: 107 miles per hour
Famous driver: Marshall Teague

★ This NASCAR winner was nicknamed the 'Fabulous Hudson Hornet' because it was almost unbeatable. In 1952, it won 83 per cent of the races it entered.

PLYMOUTH ROAD RUNNER SUPERBIRD

COOLEST CAR

Country: USA
Year introduced: 1970
Vehicle type: stock car
Engine size: 7210 cc
Top speed: 160 miles per hour
Famous driver: Richard Petty

★ A long wind-cheating nose and a tall rear spoiler made this car stand out. It also had a horn with a 'meep' sound just like the Road Runner cartoon character.

CHEVROLET LUMINA

Country: USA
Year introduced: 1989
Vehicle type: Generation 4 racer*
Engine size: 5700 cc
Top speed: over 200 miles per hour
Famous driver: Dale Earnhardt

★ This Chevrolet Lumina raced in NASCAR a full year before you could buy one to drive on the road. It was a great advertisement in front of the crowds!

42

* These are new styles of stock car introduced after NASCAR changed their design rules to make racing much safer.

Richard Petty has won the Daytona 500 race — the most important race in the NASCAR calendar — seven times. He has also been NASCAR Champion seven times. His fans call him 'the king' because of his incredible success.

TOYOTA TUNDRA

Country: USA, Japan
Year introduced: 2004
Vehicle type: Craftsman truck
Engine size: 5866 cc
Top speed: over 183 miles per hour
Famous driver: Todd Bodine

⭐ NASCAR organizes races for pick-up trucks. As Japanese manufacturer Toyota makes pick-ups in the USA, this truck could take part. It won its first race in 2004.

DODGE CHARGER

Country: USA
Year introduced: 2007
Vehicle type: Generation 5 racer*
Engine size: 5866 cc
Top speed: over 200 miles per hour
Famous driver: Kasey Kahne

⭐ In 2007, NASCAR came up with new design rules. It made this Dodge Charger much safer but still able to withstand contact with other cars in an exciting race.

FORD FUSION

Country: USA
Year introduced: 2006
Vehicle type: Generation 5 racer
Engine size: 5867 cc
Top speed: over 200 miles per hour
Famous driver: Trevor Bayne

⭐ The Ford Fusion has won the famous Daytona 500 race three times. The second victory was taken by driver Trevor Bayne, who was just 20 years old at the time.

DID YOU KNOW?
In 1930s America, drivers delivered an illegal drink called moonshine across the country. Their speedy skills, to outrun the police, led to the start of stock-car racing.

SPEED RECORDS

Imagine being the fastest driver on the planet! When you attempt the world Land Speed Record, you race against the stopwatch on a flat, empty surface. You must be absolutely fearless.

JEANTAUD

Built: France
Engine: electric motor
Record set: 1898 (twice)
Speed: 66 miles per hour
Record held for: under 1 year
Driver: Count Gaston de Chasseloup-Laubat

⭐ Chasseloup-Laubat set the first land speed record with a speed of 39.23 miles per hour. After a challenge by a rival electric car, he raised it to 66 miles per hour.

BLUEBIRD

Built: UK
Engine: aircraft piston
Record set: 1937
Speed: 301 miles per hour
Record held for: 2 months
Driver: Malcolm Campbell

⭐ Campbell set his record in this Rolls-Royce V12 aero-engined car at Bonneville Salt Flats, USA. The record was based on the average speed of two timed runs.

SPIRIT OF AMERICA SONIC 1

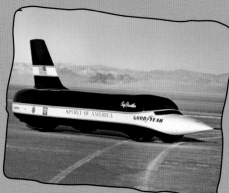

Built: USA
Engine: aircraft jet
Record set: 1965
Speed: 600 miles per hour
Record held for: 5 years
Driver: Craig Breedlove

⭐ This speed machine looked like a wingless aircraft! It passed 560 miles per hour thanks to a powerful engine from an F4 Phantom II fighter jet.

BLUE FLAME

Built: USA
Engine: rocket
Record set: 1970
Speed: 630 miles per hour
Record held for: 13 years
Driver: Gary Gabelich

⭐ The Blue Flame had only three wheels. It used a mix of liquefied natural gas and peroxide to fire a rocket engine that sent its driver streaking across the land.

THRUST SSC

LONGEST HELD

Built: UK
Engine: twin aircraft jet engines
Record set: 1997
Speed: 762 miles per hour
Record held for: 16 years plus
Driver: Andy Green

⭐ Thrust SSC was the first land-based vehicle to travel faster than the speed of sound. Andy Green set the record in the Black Rock Desert, USA, at the age of 35.

DID YOU KNOW?

In 1926, J G Parry Thomas broke the land speed record in a car named 'Babs'. One year later, the car was buried on the spot where Thomas died trying to beat his record.

BLOODHOUND SSC

Built: UK (in development)
Engine: aircraft jet and rocket
Record set: not yet attempted
Speed: up to 1,000 miles per hour
Record held for: not set
Driver: Andy Green

⭐ This 46-foot-long vehicle aims to take the land speed record over 1,000 miles per hour. The car will be more powerful than an entire grid of Formula 1 cars combined!

Donald Campbell became a record-breaker, just like his dad Malcolm. In 1964, his Proteus-Bluebird car managed a world-beating 403 miles per hour. He was the only person to become both world land and water speed champion, but later was killed in a water-speed record bid.

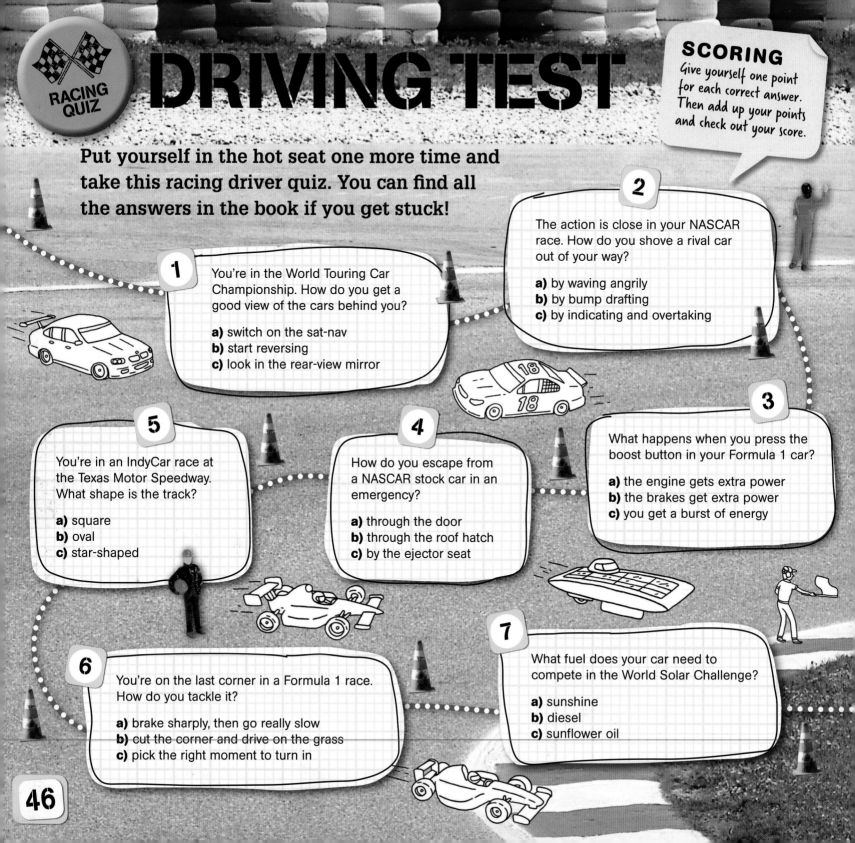

RACING QUIZ

DRIVING TEST

SCORING
Give yourself one point for each correct answer. Then add up your points and check out your score.

Put yourself in the hot seat one more time and take this racing driver quiz. You can find all the answers in the book if you get stuck!

1
You're in the World Touring Car Championship. How do you get a good view of the cars behind you?

a) switch on the sat-nav
b) start reversing
c) look in the rear-view mirror

2
The action is close in your NASCAR race. How do you shove a rival car out of your way?

a) by waving angrily
b) by bump drafting
c) by indicating and overtaking

3
What happens when you press the boost button in your Formula 1 car?

a) the engine gets extra power
b) the brakes get extra power
c) you get a burst of energy

4
How do you escape from a NASCAR stock car in an emergency?

a) through the door
b) through the roof hatch
c) by the ejector seat

5
You're in an IndyCar race at the Texas Motor Speedway. What shape is the track?

a) square
b) oval
c) star-shaped

6
You're on the last corner in a Formula 1 race. How do you tackle it?

a) brake sharply, then go really slow
b) cut the corner and drive on the grass
c) pick the right moment to turn in

7
What fuel does your car need to compete in the World Solar Challenge?

a) sunshine
b) diesel
c) sunflower oil

10

Why does your helmet have a radio link?

a) to talk to your rivals
b) to talk to your team
c) to listen to music

11

An official has just waved a yellow flag at you. What does it mean?

a) slow down
b) drive faster
c) eat a banana

12

Your dune buggy is stuck in the sand. How do you get out?

a) dig yourself out with a spade
b) accelerate as hard as you can
c) accelerate gently

How did you score?

0 – 5 Whoops! Go back to Driving School and start your training again.

6 – 9 Well done. You're roaring down the track.

10 – 12 Excellent. You've won the Championship! What car do you want to race next?

Answers
1c, 2b 3a, 4b, 5b, 6c, 7a, 8c, 9a, 10b, 11a, 12c

9

You're in the Le Mans 24 Hours driving team. How long can you drive for in one go?

a) 4 hours
b) 24 hours
c) 4 minutes

8

What should you do when you pull into the Formula 1 pits?

a) switch off the car engine
b) have a quick nap
c) stop by your garage

RACING DRIVER CERTIFICATE
CONGRATULATIONS!

You've driven different types of racing cars and you've learned the techniques that will make you a winner. See you on the start grid!

Signed

Giles Chapman

Team Manager

INDEX

accelerating 7, 9, 10–11, 16, 31

brakes and braking 7, 9, 19, 21
Brawn (Formula 1 team) 37
Button, Jenson 6, 37

Campbell, Donald 45
circuits and racetracks 18, 21, 24–25
cockpits 8–9, 27
controls 7, 9
corners and cornering 18–19, 27

Dakar Rally 30
Daytona 500 (Florida, USA) 24, 43
desert racing 30–31
drag racing 34
dune buggy 30

engines 7, 14, 15, 20, 22, 30–31, 36–45

flags 13, 25
Formula 1 6, 9, 14, 16–17, 19, 20, 36–39, 45
Formula 3 8–9
four-wheel drive 30–31, 32
funny cars 34

gears 9, 10–11
Gran Turismo racing 40

Indy Cars and the Indy 500 (Indianapolis, USA) 20–21, 38–39

karting 6–7
Kristensen, Tom 41

Hamilton, Lewis 6

Le Mans 24 Hours (France) 28–29, 40–41

Mille Miglia (Italy) 15
mirrors 8, 10–11, 27, 39

overtaking 8–9, 19

Patrick, Danica 20
pit stops 16–17, 29

racing suit 9, 12
rallies 30–31, 32–33
Red Bull (Formula 1 team) 37

Schumacher, Michael 37
single-seaters 8, 38–39
solar-powered cars and racing 34
speed 8–9, 14–15, 16, 18, 25, 27, 32
stock-car racing (including NASCAR) 22–23, 24–25, 42–43
steering and steering wheels 7, 9, 18–19, 27, 31, 32
swamp buggies 34

tactics 10–11, 25
tires 13, 16, 19, 25, 30–31
two-wheel drive 31, 32

World Touring Car Championship 26–27

CARS NAMES AND MANUFACTURERS

Alfa Romeo 15
Audi 26, 28, 41

Bentley 40
BMW 26–27
Bloodhound SSC 45
Bluebird 44
Blue Flame 45

Chevrolet 25, 42
Cobra 15

Dallara 39
Dodge 24, 34, 43

Ferrari 14, 36–37
Ford 27, 40, 43

Honda 20
Hudson Hornet 42
Hummer 31

Jaguar 41
Jeantaud 44

Kamaz 31
Kurtis-Kraft 38

Lotus 25

Maserati 36
McLaren 36
Mercedes-Benz 14, 26, 36
Miller 38
Mitsubishi 30

Penske 38
Peugeot 29, 41
Plymouth Road Runner Superbird 42
Porsche 40

Spirit of America Sonic 1 44

Thrust SSC 45
Tokal 34
Toyota 39, 43

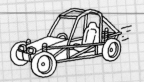